THE POLITICS OF DIVISION

THE POLITICS OF DIVISION

EMILY JO SCALZO

Five Oaks Press
FIVE-OAKS-PRESS.COM

Copyright ©2017 Emily Jo Scalzo
All rights reserved. First print edition.

Five Oaks Press
Newburgh, NY 12550
five-oaks-press.com
editor@five-oaks-press.com

ISBN: 978-1-944355-28-9

Book Design: Stacey Balkun

Printed in the United States of America

ACKNOWLEDGMENTS

Thank you to the editors of the following journals and anthologies in which these poems first appeared, some in earlier forms.

Blue Collar Review: "90% of Americans Cannot Place the Philippines on a Map"

Blue Collar Review: "Duplicity, or Why I Will Not Support Hillary Clinton"

DISARM Anthology through *Black Heart Magazine*: "Gun Control"

East Coast Literary Review: "Simulacrum Justice"

Mobius: The Journal of Social Change: "Postcards to Whitman from Cuba"

Mobius: The Journal of Social Change: "Stardust"

New Verse News: "Higher Education Held Hostage"

Scarlet Leaf Review: "If the Human Race is the Only Race, Why Does this Shit Still Happen?"

Scarlet Leaf Review: "The Reason I Blocked You on Facebook"

Scarlet Leaf Review: "To My Father"

Perspective Literary Magazine: "Revisionist History, Compliments Texas Board of Education"

Contents

To My Father	5
Postcards to Whitman from Cuba	7
Higher Education Held Hostage	20
If the Human Race is the Only Race, Why Does this Shit Still Happen?	21
90% of Americans Cannot Place the Philippines on a Map	22
Simulacrum Justice	24
Gun Control	25
Depressions of a News Junkie	26
The Rhetoric of Power	27
College Composition	28
Revisionist History, Compliments Texas Board of Education	29
Duplicity, or Why I Will Not Support Hillary Clinton	30
Continued News from Deepwater Horizon	31
America Spent 2015 at Half-Staff	32
Superfund IV	33
What the Heart Dreams	34
The Status of Freedom in Modern America	35
Channeling Ginsberg on Contemporary American Politics	36
The Reason I Blocked You on Facebook	37
Bilingual	38
Stardust	39
Hear America Sing	40

To My Father

For Stephen Michael Scalzo
September 12, 1943 – November 16, 2016
Rest in Peace, Daddy

I've never told you
I secretly check your breathing at night,
listening in the dark
if you're not snoring when I go to the bathroom.

I was on the phone five years ago
all the way in Fresno, when Mom said,
"Oh, God, your father just fell off the roof,"
and hung up, leaving me in static.

You're the only person I know who, in his sixties,
would still climb up on his mother-in-law's roof
in a tornado-producing Midwest rainstorm
to clean her overflowing gutters.

I waited for the call only to learn you were stubborn,
lying on Grandma's couch insisting you were fine,
when in fact three vertebrae had been broken.
You would be on disability for months.

When I flew in for my birthday
you met me in the airport, called my name.
I didn't recognize you, dismissed you
as speaking to someone who shared my name.

You were never old in my eyes until that moment.
You had stopped shaving because it hurt too much,
had a full beard, mostly salt with a bit of pepper,
when I'd only ever seen you clean-shaven in all my life.

It was the summer Mom got the dogs—
one, at first, and then five when she gave birth,
then back down to two again—
company while you sat at home in your hard plastic shell.

Five years later, your back wakes you,
and you spend nights on the couch in the living room.
You're too feeble to even lift the fallen
pink throw pillow sewn by your mother.

When I pick it up for you, you hold it
like a child might hold a teddy bear,
and fall right to sleep, leaving me
to listen for your breathing from my room.

Postcards to Whitman from Cuba

1.

In the elevator of the Peters building at Fresno State,
A young man in a wheelchair wears a shirt of Che Guevara circled
       in red,
Crossed out,
The slash like blood across his face.
I want to ask him about it, wish I was wearing my own Che shirt,
As though it might spark a rational conversation.
I wonder if he is Cuban,
If he is against la Revolución or just communism.
Is he against the man or the symbol?
Does he even know what it means?

2.

Dear Walt,
Did you know at state functions, Fidel Castro had your poetry read,
And your songs have inspired many a communist?
You and your poetry inspired José Martí,
Perhaps even brought about his poetry during the Ten Years' War,
Enflamed him and other young Cubans to fight for independence
    from Spain.
They won it after your death, and his, long after he met you in New
    York.
Did they translate his adoration of you before you died?
I wonder if, much later, your songs inspired two young men to take
    Cuba from a dictator,
Only to become a different kind of tyrant.
I doubt you meant them to become what they defeated,
But you also expected Cuba would be one of the fifty states.

I have been there, Walt, to see what Cuba means after la Revolución
With my own eyes.
I have photographs in my mind,
Beauty and sensation impossible to capture on any film,
And I return there sometimes in sleep or daydreams.
I can see why you wanted Cuba's beauty to be America's.

3.

Che's grave is silent, a mausoleum.
No pictures allowed; our cameras are taken by soldiers before we enter.
Six years later, I rely on memory to see it.
I can no longer recall if the plants inside were real or silk, only that they were a vibrant green, an ivy trailing all over.
The familiar visage, uncrossed, stares out at me, carved in metal on the wall
With the names of comrades who died in Bolivia with him,
Fighting for a utopic vision of egalitarianism,
A Latin American future free of imperialism and rampant poverty.
He told his killers they could only kill a man,
His ideals would live forever.

His face is the face of Cuba, painted on buildings and billboards everywhere,
More of a father to the nation than Castro.
Che's name means revolution, his face freedom.
The official monument to Che stands in Santa Clara.
A carved block of white stone depicts his life and an eternal flame burns within.
His true monument is Cuba,
La Revolución that lives on, immortal as he wished,
Twisted, perhaps, but intact in the hearts of the Cuban people.

After seeing Che's grave,
We sit in the center of a hotel built to resemble a collection of thatch huts, gather under the eaves while it rains,
Watch hummingbirds flit in the flowered trees,
Smell the renewal of the earth,
Drink mojitos and Cuba Libres, and smoke cigars in the twilight.
Would you sit and drink and smoke with us, Walt?
Or would you go out into the rain and let it soak into your beard?

4.

In Habana, we drive el Malecón,
Past the United States Interests Section and the José Martí Anti-Imperialist Plaza.
A dark metal statue,
Martí's imposing figure holding a child protectively and pointing at the building.
A glimpse only, caught from our moving bus.
Our tour guide explains in detail, but it amounts to one word:
Elián.

Later, the salty air rushes through the cab to blow our hair back and caress our faces,
Our cabbies drag-racing down el Malecón,
Taking us back to our hotel from Old Habana where we had dinner at El Floridita and toasted Hemingway.
There is joy in the race, in the free feeling of sea air.
We stick our faces close to the open windows
And laugh into the wind.

When we walk el Malecón, a woman scares off the young man trying to woo me in a mix of Spanish, English, and Italian.
She tells us Cubans are evil, not to be trusted,
And in the next breath asks for our addresses, so she may write to us when we return to the US,
Proudly listing the countries she writes,
While I listen to the sea pound against the wall in the dark and sprinkle us with a mist of saltwater,
And watch children down the way hop the wall to play on the rocks near the ocean.
I expect you would be among them, Walt.

5.

The trees have dropped the mangos outside of Hemingway's house,
And people gather them up to eat.
Children in school uniforms play in the jagüey trees along streets in
      Habana, root systems above the ground like vines, perfect to
           climb and hide in.
We lie in the center of a pavilion over a koi pond in a Japanese-style
      garden, a circle of faces for a photograph,
And sip guava juice in a cool pine forest with a soft blanket of pine
      needles under our feet in the National Botanical Gardens.
In an urban garden the earth stains our shoes and feet red, and I
      long to walk barefoot between the rows of plants,
To grind the dirt into my skin and hold Cuba forever.

At the Agrarian University, students dance and stomp in street
      clothes
In an open space on cracked tile to Cuban pop echoing down
      the hall, their bodies waving in ways that look both natural
           and practiced.
They show us labs where they work on biotechnology and grow
      better plants through selective breeding.
Afterward we walk in a field of long grass toward the buildings.
One is crumbled and unfinished; the land is taking it back.
The Russians were building it, they tell us, and then the USSR fell.
We sit in the grass with Cuban students and play with the sensitive
      plants,
Touch them to make their leaves wither and fold inward, then wait
      for them to open again.

6.

Our only Sunday in Habana, we go to a rumba in a painted alley,
Callejón de Hamel,
A well-known place in which the music lasts all day.
A hot throng of people sweat and dance.
A little girl, a mix of African and Indian and Spanish heritage, her face
    wet with the sheen of sweat and her dark curls dusty,
Walks among the tourists holding up a silver three-peso coin
    embossed on one side with Che's face, patria o muerte,
Looking to trade for an American dollar.
Young men illegally sell CDs of the music until the police come and
    make them stop.
The child disappears into the crowd with two quarters for her peso.

Standing on the uneven cobblestones of El Morro, I look out across
    the bay at the Habana skyscape,
What could be an American city viewed through the morning mist on
    the water.
I wonder how soldiers could run in the castle without breaking an
    ankle or falling.
I walk through archways that seem to rise to accommodate giants
And I feel insignificant.
At another El Morro, on the other end of the island, I look over a wall
    at a scene that belongs on a postcard,
A white shoreline fading one way into vibrant green, mountains
    jutting into a perfect blue sky with clouds like a painting,
And the other way into an ocean so blue it looks unreal.
The Caribbean coast as viewed from El Morro in Santiago de Cuba,
On high walls so thick you can lie across them
And look over the edge to a sheer drop into dream-blue ocean that
    pounds against stone.

7.

Limestone mogotes, bumps of green, rise from deep tan tobacco fields,
A scent that wafts up to the balcony of my hotel room in Las Viñales where I stand,
Leaning against the rail into the vision as you must have when you came to Cuba, though your visit almost certainly predates this hotel.
Up close on a tobacco farm, they no longer jut into the sky,
But rise majestically, a mosaic of white and green and yellow.
The farmer shows us the tobacco dryer, a triangle-shaped shed with leaves of tobacco drying on poles.
He hands me a leaf, and I smuggle it back with me, encase it in plastic, and every so often take it out and smell and remember.
He shows us his car, a mint-condition 1950 Cadillac, turns on the radio, and dances with us,
While we take turns going inside to buy illegal cigars the family makes with surplus tobacco and sells to tourists.
It is his son's birthday, and our professor produces a roll of Lifesavers.
The boy flushes and grins with it held in his fist as we sing Happy Birthday to him.

Down the road in a building that serves as a school in daylight hours, we watch the sun set behind a mogote through slatted windows,
The glare blinding us, bleeding against the wall
Until it sinks low enough.
Here we meet a Comité de Defensa de la Revolución, Che's immortality in the people of the neighborhood,
Making sure everyone gets enough to eat, the sick are cared for, and everyone does their part.

When I describe it to my mother, she will ask, "What if someone doesn't want to?"
I don't understand the question.
Am I a communist, Walt?
Are you, who believed all souls equal?

8.

We find ourselves at a tourist trap,
A cave where the guides dress like Native Americans and take us
 through on a boat.
Afterward we go downstream where Cubans are swimming in gentle
 rapids.
I sit on a rock in the middle of the stream and watch the children play,
Soak my feet in the cool clear water and let the minnows nibble my
 toes.
If I were to float on my back like a piece of wood, I wonder where it
 would take me.
Underground or over a cliff? Would it bob me along all the way to the
 ocean?
Perhaps you know now, Walt, part of those pent-up aching rivers.

At an old coffee plantation once run by the French, we push the wheel
 as slaves once did to separate the beans from their shells
And find it too heavy for even three of us.
Our professor finds a live termite hive attached to the side of a Spanish
 cedar,
And breaks bits off,
Lets the termites crawl on his hands.
He tells us a termite hive operates as communism was supposed to,
 everyone with a purpose—
These termites are the first defense against invasion, spraying
 chemicals on his hands to scare him off.
"But people aren't termites," someone says,
And Bob replies, "That's the problem."
If we stay, he tells us, the next wave of defense is flying stinging
 ones.
We race down the hill as though they are already after us,
Your hand in mine as we try not to slip in the eroded dirt of
 what was once a road.

9.

In Habana, we meet a woman who moved from the US to Cuba after
    la Revolución,
The wife of a revolutionary.
The ration card she passes around reminds me of the card for
    collecting subscription money when I delivered newspapers.
We sit by the hotel pool, and she tells of working for the Cuban
    Ministry of Agriculture,
Breakthroughs she oversaw, projects that died with the USSR, and
    the struggle during the Special Period.
Farmers turned to organic, she tells us, to survive without pesticides.
The chlorine from the pool burns my eyes, and the reflection of light
    from the water plays across her face.
She breaks off to tell us of coming to the US to give birth to her
    autistic son,
Of going through labor during the Cuban Missile Crisis, wondering
    if Cuba would be there when she was ready to return.
I wonder now how she reacted to Raúl Castro's reworking of
    agriculture,
If she agrees the communist system was an inefficient shackle.
I wonder how you might react to all I have experienced here, Walt,
    what Cuba is today.

When we visit her son at a mental hospital, a self-sufficient complex
    where patients grow their own food,
He smiles when we tell him we know his mother,
Looking up from the hat he is making from the dried leaf sheath of
    the royal palm
That will eventually go home with a tourist.
He tells us in a thick voice, in Spanish, that Jimmy Carter shook his
    hand,
And he has the picture to prove it.
The woman who runs the hospital sits with us under a canopy of
    trees and serves us fresh juice made from the mango trees
    cultivated on the grounds.
When we ask if she has visited the US she recounts being a
    passenger on a hijacked plane,
Of wanting to get back home to her patients in Cuba,
As you must have wanted to return to the hospitals where your
    soldiers were dying.

10.

Camagüey is a maze of a city built to confuse pirates, to separate
    them so they could be cut down.
It is my birthday, and I am happy to just be in Cuba,
But the hotel surprises me by making a huge cake with icing made
    from real sugar, with a gritty texture, so much sweeter than
    I could make it here.
They serve it with strawberry ice cream and a bottle of champagne.
A Haitian group invites us to their rehearsal at an art gallery.
Afterwards they sing Happy Birthday to me in four languages,
And we walk back to the hotel in the cool night air, the stars
    winking at us.
In the bar, you hand me a cigar, Walt.

On the way to Bayamo, the bus runs over a rock placed in the road
    to warn motorists of upcoming roadwork,
And we stop for repairs in Las Tunas, a sleepy town, where we see
    no bar or tourist attractions.
We are disappointed by the lack of alcohol—
After learning all proceeds of sales to tourists went to restoring
    historical buildings, we vowed to drink enough to restore
    an entire building on our own,
And we view this as a missed opportunity.
We sit on a concrete porch in the shade and play Euchre for hours,
    ignored by the locals.
We are appeased in Bayamo, for the original city was burned to the
    ground in the Ten Years' War,
And what little remains of the original is covered in a ten-minute
    walking tour.
There is nothing to do in Bayamo but drink.

11.

We walk the streets of Santiago de Cuba, slipping into little shops littering the area, spending the last of our money on artwork and souvenirs and gifts.
Last night we took an illegal cab from downtown to our hotel, the driver whipping through side streets,
Taking us the way real cabs never would, through the gritty parts of the city.
We went to the hotel across the street, the expensive one, with a bar on the top floor,
And saw teenage Cuban girls dressed in skimpy outfits, making money with their bodies from the tourists.
Outside our hotel, a woman without teeth shows us she has lost a flip-flop and begs for change.
The next time we see her, she has found it.
We go to a beach generally used by locals only, a beach with tiny stones instead of sand, and we play in the water and get sunburns.
There is a heat in the city that was absent from Habana, less tempered by the Caribbean bay than Habana Bay on the Atlantic,
But the air still has moisture that makes our hair curl and frizz.

We sit around the hotel pool and drink eight bottles of rum with our professors.
Bob continues stories that started in Bayamo and ended when we were too drunk to hear them, he too drunk to tell them,
About the jobs he has held, his Boston accent, and the places he's traveled.
None of us know in four years, scattered across the world, we will drink or smoke a toast in his honor
When cancer takes him,
And I will remember him standing among the fragrant cedars and ghostly pines and shadowy mahogany trees,
Invading a termite nest with a look of boyish glee.
Tonight we don't know that future, but we drink rum and smoke cigars as though it is our last night on earth,
Because it is our last night in Cuba.

12.

It was in Habana, at the Agrarian University, where we banded
 together as a community,
We American students abroad.
At the guest house, they served us traditional lunches
Of beans and rice and plantains and other delicious foods, with fresh
 fruit juice—pineapple, guava, passion fruit.
You would have enjoyed it, Walt.
We shared our plates, no one going hungry, eating from each other's
 like siblings, except even siblings don't do that anymore,
Relaxing afterward during the heat of the day, catching the little
 lizards that came to sun themselves on the brick and
 releasing them again.
We did this at all the hotels thereafter, leaving nothing to throw away.

When we arrive back in Miami after the trip, Denny's is a strange
 experience.
Three groups of us, seated around the restaurant,
Calling back and forth between the tables,
"Hey, do you want my fries?"
"Anyone interested in my tomato?"
"You going to eat that?"
The waitress looks at us like we are crazy, until we tell her we just flew
 back from Cuba.
"I'm from there," she tells us. "I understand."
But I don't know if she does,
This joy in being together, in sharing what we have to make everyone
 happy, of being nourished by this sense of community we've
 never felt before,
Gathered around our own chowder-kettle,
Or if she just understands a different kind of hunger.

You should have been with us that night.
We would have shared with complete strangers,
Would have asked you, Walt, to sit with us and partake of our
 communal pot.
There was plenty for everyone,
Too much for just us.

13.

Do you whisper hasta la victoria siempre in the night?
Is this the soft-breath'd Cuba you saw and wanted as a state?
Are these your reasons?
Is it the same Cuba that appears in my dreams, these snapshots
    of scent and sensation,
This feeling of belonging,
These memories that float to the surface and sear the mind with
    longing?
Do you wake from these dreams with tears on your cheeks, too?
And feel the pull of the magic of the island,
Though we can never go back?

Higher Education Held Hostage

The parking lot at Chicago State University
overflowed the night before the announcement
of nine hundred staff layoffs, a death knell—
the result of the budget impasse in Springfield.

Bernie Sanders chose this venue to hold a rally,
a state university now decimated by political gridlock,
its demographic comprised largely of minorities—
the latest victim in our sad culture war.

After eight months without state funding,
Spring Break was axed to finish the semester early,
to allow seniors to complete degrees, graduate—
all other students in limbo, the river run dry.

At twelve I haunted the halls of Chicago State University,
playing hooky from my small-town middle school,
attending my first poetry reading outside the president's office—
surrounded by Ebonics and Spanish, African and Latin art.

There I was embraced in culture and pride in diversity,
political protests, creative endeavors, intellectual encouragement;
this environment, a refuge, determined my future—
soon those halls will be walked only by ghosts.

If the Human Race is the Only Race, Why Does this Shit Still Happen?

#AllLivesMatter makes me want
to flay my skin from my body,
strip by pale strip
to offer to my brethren
who were born without
the benefit of lazy melanin.

Times like these I hate
the liberty I was born to,
have benefitted from,
continue to possess,
allowing me to live without
fear I'll be shot if I'm pulled over.

If—I probably won't be stopped
if I don't signal a turn quickly enough,
have a broken taillight,
fit a profile or vague suspect description,
look "bad" or "on something,"
or am just in the wrong neighborhood.

I wish we white people could see
the damage we do to bodies of color
but cognitive dissonance
slices deep and most prefer ignorance
to agonized awareness of the fortune
we enjoy by accident.

So we falsely invoke Dr. King,
whitewash him for our purposes,
pretending we'd approve of him
while shaming #BlackLivesMatter
for the same direct action
as they fight his same battles

against similar demagogues
because we can't learn from history,

doomed to repeat ad nauseum
the sins of our forefathers
against our fellows of the human race,
ignoring our privilege to protect it.

90% of Americans Cannot Place the Philippines on a Map

It's the strongest ever recorded hitting landfall,
known as Super Typhoon Haiyan,
but mention it to many Americans
and you receive blank stares.

The news making radar
involves Incognito and the Dolphins,
bullying and racism in the locker room,
his insistence he said what he did out of love.

Or the plagiarism scandal engulfing Rand Paul
and his desire to duel Rachel Maddow,
were it still legal in the state of Kentucky,
for daring to break the story.

Meanwhile, estimated ten thousand people dead,
four and a half million homeless,
a swath of destruction compared to a tsunami,
bloated bodies rotting in the street,

not enough body bags to hold them all,
children crying for food and water,
rain lashing a people with no shelter left,
desperately crowding the airport to leave—

for days get a footnote in the American media,
and, soon after the blip, are forgotten.

Simulacrum Justice

When Obama pardons nonviolent drug offenders
whose sentences would be lighter under current law
my Facebook feed lights up predictably,
right wingers calling foul—one comparing
drug offenders to murderers and rapists,
others offering speculation on ethnicity,
racial stereotypes, and slurs.

The practice of the pardon and commuted sentence
is one this President has rarely used when compared
to previous presidents—Wikipedia's 'List of people
pardoned by George W. Bush' is longer by far
and largely populated by white collar criminals;
are detractors protesting the nature of the crime,
or the presumed social status of the criminal?

Drug laws are antiquated,
widely discussed in media and politics
as targeting the lowest socioeconomic rung
far more harshly than the higher—
drug crime convictions 'favor' the poor,
the non-white, those hooked on drugs
not out of suburban boredom.

The real crime isn't the President's pardons,
but a system which lets the Ethan Couches
of the nation get away with murder or fraud
serving time at luxury rehab clinics or
prisons with golf courses and air conditioning,
while plebe convicts suffer the subhuman conditions
of a for-profit justice system whose inmates can't pay.

I will never understand those friends politically,
but their tones invite no discussion—
they believe the justice system is solely
for punishment, not rehabilitation,
which they believe impossible—
and the only recourse is clicking
'I don't want to see this' and moving on.

Gun Control

When I see the news trending—
a kindergartener found a gun,
fatally shot his 9-month-old brother
in his own crib, an accident,
my immediate reaction is grief.

The boy will grow up knowing
the brother he was meant
to protect died by his hand—
regardless of the circumstances,
what will that do to his psyche?

It mixes with anger at parents
who left a gun in reach of a child,
but also pity, knowing they
will spend their lives regretting
gun safety education through tragedy.

And the thought I suppress,
but which bubbles up anyway—

"Is the answer to this more guns, too?"

Depressions of a News Junkie

A Yazidi mother forced to leave her young disabled son in the baking
    desert sun as IS forces shoot, close in;
the children of Gaza walking in rubble-strewn filthy streets with the
    uncertain ceasefire end looming;
a convoy of evacuees in Ukraine fired on by rockets, an unknown
    number dead, failing to flee the war;
the world media tires of reporting the carnage in Syria, even as more
    are massacred, tortured, displaced;
youth killed under questionable circumstances on American streets
    by police charged to serve and protect;
ethnic cleansing, neighbor murdering neighbor, Christian vs.
    Muslim, in the Central African Republic;

and beyond the human,
(though caused by humans):
climate change ruin,
more elephants poached than born,
groundwater polluted with methane,
Amazon rainforest logged to oblivion,
the impending destruction of the Great Barrier Reef...

Being human is hard
when you'd prefer
not to be associated
with human behavior.

The Rhetoric of Power

The soundbytes tell us
left is progressive,
right is traditional,
liberal, conservative,
two sides of a coin;
but they are the currency,
and the rest of the world
is reality.

College Composition

Students arrive bathed in contagion spread
by media and figureheads,
believing arguments can be won through
brute strength and ignorance,
the idea that rational discussion is weakness,
when in reality no one is guaranteed an audience
and silence is not a sign of acquiescence.

I attempt to disabuse them of this idea
the first few weeks of every semester,
undo the damage done by
a society bathed in conflict—
words replacing fists, with similar consequences—
unravel the agonism seen as critical thinking,
although I fear I fight a losing battle.

Revisionist History, Compliments Texas Board of Education

Thomas Jefferson was not a founding father,
cut from the curriculum,
his ideas too liberal for young minds
even as prayer takes place
before high school football games
and those young minds learn of Jesus,
more progressive than Jefferson.
Instead of a nation,
he founded a religion.
No asterisk on the cross,
bringing salvation for all.
But, like Jefferson in schools,
Christ is left out of the sermons
in Texas.

Duplicity, or Why I Will Not Support Hillary Clinton

At eight I campaigned for Perot over Clinton
during the faux elections at my elementary school.

As a child I didn't trust that smile,
just wide enough to feel false.

My true dislike of the Clintons came much later,
when in college I learned about NAFTA,

saw Bill betray his base with his predecessor
patting his back as he signed without alteration,

betraying the working class who had voted for him
after he had promised provisions to protect their jobs.

Later I learned of the genocide in Rwanda,
watched the news clips of his Press Secretary

quibbling over how many 'acts of genocide'
constitute genocide, and the meaning of 'is,'

while 800,000 were massacred by machete
and principles were abandoned for convenience.

Perhaps I shouldn't find Hillary guilty of Bill's crimes,
but her record as Senator was more of the same.

Like a snake she sheds her skin when politic,
becoming whatever will garner the most donations,

a career politician basing convictions on focus groups;
forked tongue hidden until too late.

Continued News from Deepwater Horizon

A spiral of oil spread toward the bayous visible from space,
A man-o-war floating on a sea of rust,
decomposing turtles washing up on beaches,
nesting pelicans crowding a scrub-covered dune in the path of
      the sludge.

The spiral, the day after, was the size of Rhode Island
and a day later the size of West Virginia.
Dispersal chemicals prevented measurement after,
but oil still pumped into the ocean.

Originally this was called an impossibility,
no contingency plan existed.
Now the plan includes paying a pittance to victims not to sue
and sweeping beaches to remove tar balls.

America looks at mining disasters in China and says,
"That's communism for you,"
but lately pipeline ruptures here are commonplace,
and poisonous dust invades homes from refineries.

Now swimmers leave the Gulf with oil sheen polluting their skin,
and the region still bleeds toxic plume fallout,
while BP seeks to block claims to its pitiful fund for damages,
claiming fraud by those drowned by corporate greed,

disputes the study funded by them which found
gulf dolphins are dying in droves, lung disease and
other abnormalities, signs of toxic oil contamination,
claims there is no connection to the oil spill.

Still tar balls are combed from the sand,
nearly five million pounds in 2013 alone,
tar mats buried under sediment by tropical storms,
dug up and carried away by the truck-load.

America Spent 2015 at Half-Staff

Obama ordered the American flag lowered
in response to San Bernardino,
one mass shooting of too many.

The stars and stripes should be depressed
every day for the next 355
for the sake of consistency.

Or perhaps we should flip the flag,
display our SOS, our cry for help,
acknowledge our nation in crisis.

Superfund IV

They let poison drip
into the veins of Americana,
a slow-acting draught
of heavy metal contaminant,
an orange slurry
of corrosion and bacteria,
leaving a generation's
brains weighted
and futures dimmed.

What the Heart Dreams

I was stuck in traffic
in what appeared to be
a suburban area,

the kind a little worn
weathered,
working class.

No one was moving,
and then Bernie Sanders appeared,
shaking hands through car windows,

wearing a jean-blue
heathered button-up shirt
with a stain on the collar.

He saw me looking at it.
"It's mustard from lunch," he told me.
"There's this great deli up the street."

His hand was warm,
his grip firm and friendly,
his smile welcoming and honest.

The traffic jammed street
became an impromptu rally,
and the enigmatic socialist

in his stained blue-collar shirt
spoke to us like comrades
in a middle-class wasteland.

The Status of Freedom in Modern America

A woman lay in the street
her face red-splotched
tearstained and in pain
screaming it burns, it burns—
pepper-sprayed because her sign
read "#BlackLivesMatter"
and the police don't agree.

A man pushed to the icy ground
forced to lay there in the cold
while the police handcuff him
for saying "I can't breathe" too loudly.
They keep him on the concrete
as people yell at them to stop
and let him up before he freezes.

Tear gas in the middle
of a parking lot, preventing
protesters from leaving.
They run from their cars
their faces tear-streaked
as they try to escape the fumes,
abused for wanting justice.

CNN claims protesters rioted
yet they were peaceful,
victims of a city intolerant
of differing opinions.
Only witnesses know the truth,
labeled disturbers of the peace
for daring to speak out.

Channeling Ginsberg on Contemporary American Politics

Howl into the echoing void of empty rhetoric polluting what was once
    balanced political discourse replaced with putrid nattering
Staining young minds with shit spewed by mayfly politicians born to
    lazy opulence or cheating their way there on the bent spines
        of plebes
Who have never struggled or who have at least forgotten the struggle
    of life lived by paltry paycheck, hungry and desperate
Fighting and clawing for funds from bloated billionaires for cockamamie
    campaigns full of empty promises and annoying emails
Mired in rancid pork with over 100 vacation days, paid time off,
    protected pensions, heavenly healthcare—taxpayer funded—
The tattered remnants of 1950s middle class America gifted to dullards
    who do no work but for the seated, silent, absent filibuster
And complain of low pay in the face of the impoverished, skimming off
    the top, accepting lobbyist bribes, handjobs under desks
Hiding favors received by Wall Street behind a transparent curtain while
    pretending compassion for the needs of the peasants
Catamites to the conceited czars of capitalism, sucking deep on the
    parched teat of luxury afforded to those with corporate
        connections
Ignoring the plight of constituents mired in vacuous ignorance and
    bottomless debt and duped into voting between pricks,
The naïve 20% left who believe in the crippled system enough to cast
    a hope and prayer on Election Day for better than this shit
But are consistently disappointed with dregs of humanity, the
    questionably sane willing to run for the degrading position
Involving constant scrutiny, puerile nonsense, dehumanizing bombast,
    speaking of nothing through insults and fallacy
Of top asshole, least nauseating to those few who bother to cast their
    dreams away—or at least most skilled in gerrymandering—
Who gets to choose the strap-on with which to fuck the American public
    and American Constitution and American Dream
For the next four years.

The Reason I Blocked You on Facebook

I don't feel like playing nice anymore,
plying proper rhetoric
while you spew hyperbole,
my voice lost in the vacuum
public discourse has become.
Baited with insults and slander,
you try to tempt me with demagoguery,
never listening unless I snap
and then only to point at my lost temper,
believing it a sign you've won,
that discussion is a battle one can win,
and it's like fighting a monolith
formed of excrement and bile,
an exercise in futility
destined to end in disease.

Bilingual

My earliest memory
is splashing in a pool
in Cancun at age two
with a boy who knew
a different tongue
but spoke the language
of play.

Stardust

Aurorae over the blanket of Ganymede
tell of ocean under 100 miles of ice,
of the potential for life we can recognize,
close, in galactic terms, to home,
more within reach than distant stars.

Liquid water discovered
under the icy surface of moons,
warmed by gravitational friction,
Jupiter and Saturn their suns,
tantalize us with possibilities.

As we look out on the mess of Earth,
seven billion locusts swarming;
something better must be out there,
just far enough that
we can't taint it.

Hear America Sing

O Whitman! my Whitman!
If you could see the America of today I wonder what you would think,
We people glued to our devices that show us nature through glass—in HD so our crippled imaginations do not have to grapple with uncertainty.
We do not have to be in it and touch it and lay with it.
Our children do not wonder What is the grass?—only What is on television?
The hum of the machines that engirth us has music in it, a never-ending cacophony that sometimes seems symphonic.
We never truly listen to hear it.
We do not love it.

The political landscape, so similar in ways but different—so different—from your own.
The death of a President shaped your life...
Perhaps you would be more drawn to the sixties,
With its free giving and taking of sex and pleasures of all kinds, body and spirit and everything in between,
And the death of its own dynamic hero, shot dead as the nation looked on in horror.

Those soldiers you saw, dead in droves,
Those fine men you comforted and grieved over...
Would you believe we have become more efficient killers?
That six million people were killed in six years, and America did nothing for two of them?
That a million people were hacked to death in one hundred days while our leaders debated the definition of genocide?
That in an instant your America removed eighty thousand souls from the world, and did so more than once, and planned to do so again and again if we did not get our way?
American bunkers keep enough weapons to destroy the world hundreds of times over,
And still we make more.

Would you despise our priests now?
Those who molest children... Those who call to bomb abortion

clinics… Those who kill in the name of Allah and God
and Yahweh and Brahmin and all others…
Those who set themselves on fire to protest,
Or spill gallons of blood donated milliliter by milliliter on the steps
of a palace,
Or round up all those they find offensive in race or religion or creed—
real or imagined—to maim and murder them with gas or
bomb or gun or machete,
Or strive to impose their will on others through violence or legislature,
Or who reject atheists and Jews and Muslims and all the Eastern
religions as subservient (or worse) to Christianity—
Their Christianity, in which God is in their image and their Christ
spread messages of hate instead of love, and died only for
those select perfect.
His sacrament burns like acid down the throat.

Those were there in your time too, but you saw past them.
Could you see past them now?

Perhaps your faith, the greatest of faiths and the least of faiths,
That poetry of your soul, encompassing everything ancient and of
your time and even the future that is now,
Perhaps that is what we are missing.
Can you perhaps come again upon the earth a bit sooner than five
thousand years?
Do the oracles and gods and sun tell you what has come to pass,
Or are you part of the grass now,
Or in a world spawned by your songs, the America of hopes and
dreams and whispered wishes?

You have left on your journey and not returned
And the teabaggers have taken your place.
Discordant voices spread disharmony and lies, manufacture hatred
and greed and suffering for mass-consumption,
Protestors at the funerals of soldiers,
Celebration of murder and violence and hate for ideological gain.
Patriotism turned vitriolic.

Those who walk without sympathy lure the armies of those you
        love into their coffins unchecked.
We no longer know how to celebrate ourselves.

O Whitman! our Whitman! come sing upon the earth again,
Engirth us and discorrupt us,
Recharge our souls,
And teach us the song of America again.

www.ingramcontent.com/pod-product-compliance
Lightning Source LLC
Chambersburg PA
CBHW071758080526
44588CB00013B/2285